STRASBOURG

CHRISTMAS MARKETS 2024-2025

*Explore The City's Xmas Bazaars And Have
A Memorable Holiday Experience During
The Festive Season*

NATASHA D. VARNEY

TABLE OF CONTENTS

Map Of Strasbourg

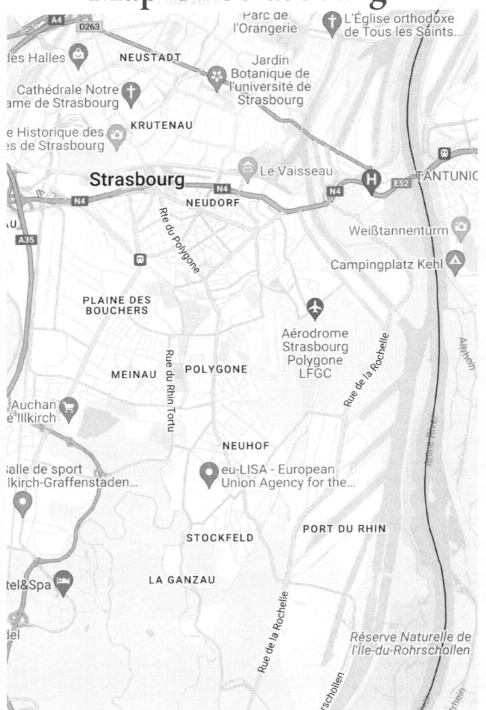

INTRODUCTION

As the plane descended over the picturesque city of Strasbourg, I felt a flutter of excitement in my chest. The anticipation of experiencing the world-renowned Christmas markets had been building for months, and now, here I was, about to embark on a journey that promised to be nothing short of magical.

Stepping off the plane, the crisp winter air greeted me, carrying with it the faint scent of mulled wine and roasted chestnuts. Strasbourg, often referred to as the "Capital of Christmas," was already living up to its name. The streets were adorned with twinkling lights, and the festive spirit was palpable.

My first stop was the Christkindelsmärik, the oldest Christmas market in France, dating back to 1570. As I wandered through the labyrinth of wooden stalls, each one brimming with handcrafted ornaments, delicious treats, and unique gifts, I couldn't help but feel like a child again, wide-eyed and full of wonder. The market was a sensory delight —the vibrant colors, the cheerful sounds of carolers, and the mouthwatering aromas of traditional Alsatian cuisine created an atmosphere that was both enchanting and heartwarming.

One of the highlights of my visit was the breathtaking Strasbourg Cathedral, its Gothic spires reaching towards the heavens. The cathedral's façade was illuminated by a stunning light show, casting a magical glow over the entire square. Inside, the nativity scene was a masterpiece of artistry, depicting the story of Christmas with intricate detail and reverence.

As I strolled through the cobblestone streets of Petite France, the historic quarter of Strasbourg, I was transported back in time. The half-timbered houses, adorned with festive decorations, looked like something out of a fairy tale. The gentle hum of the River Ill added to the serene ambiance, making it the perfect place to reflect on the true meaning of the season.

One evening, I found myself at Place Kléber, where the Great Christmas Tree stood tall and proud. Surrounded by families and friends, all gathered to celebrate the joy of Christmas, I felt a profound sense of connection and community. It was a reminder that, no matter where we come from, the spirit of Christmas has the power to bring us all together.

As Christmas Eve approached, the city seemed to glow even brighter. The anticipation of the big day was in the air, and the markets were bustling with last-minute shoppers. I spent the evening savoring a cup of spiced wine, watching the snowflakes dance in the air, and listening to the joyous sounds of a nearby choir. It was a moment of pure bliss, one that I will cherish forever.

Writing this book has been a labor of love, a way to share the magic of Strasbourg's Christmas markets with you. Whether you're planning your first visit or returning for another dose of festive cheer, I hope this guide will help you navigate the markets, discover hidden gems, and create memories that will last a lifetime. So, bundle up, grab a warm drink, and join me on this enchanting journey through the heart of Christmas.

CHAPTER 1

Brief History Of Strasbourg Christmas Markets

Origins And Early Years

The origins of the Strasbourg Christmas markets can be traced back to the late 12th century when the city held a Klausenmärik (Saint Nicolas market) every year on December 6th. This market was a place for locals to stock up on provisions for the holiday season. However, with the advent of Protestantism in the Alsace region, the market underwent a significant transformation. In 1570, the Klausenmärik was replaced by the Christkindelsmärik, or "Market of the Christ Child," which shifted the focus from Saint Nicholas to the Christkind, an angel-like figure from Alsatian folklore who symbolizes the spirit of Christmas and brings gifts to children.

Evolution And Expansion

Initially, the Christkindelsmärik was held only for three days before Christmas Eve. However, as the market grew in popularity, its duration was extended. By the second half of the 19th century, the market was held for 36 days, significantly longer than its original three-day span. This expansion allowed for a greater variety of goods and activities, transforming the market into a major event in the city's calendar.

Cultural Significance

The Strasbourg Christmas markets have played a pivotal role in shaping the region's holiday spirit. The markets are not just a place for commerce but a celebration of Alsatian culture and traditions. The emphasis on authenticity, featuring handmade crafts, local delicacies, and festive decorations, has helped preserve and promote the unique cultural heritage of the region.

Modern-Day Markets

Today, the Strasbourg Christmas markets are a sprawling wonderland of festive lights, artisanal stalls, and local food products. The markets are spread throughout the city center, with the main market located in Place Broglie. Other notable markets include those at Place de la Cathédrale, Place Kléber, and Place Gutenberg. Each market has its unique theme and offerings, from traditional Alsatian crafts to international goods, making Strasbourg a melting pot of festive cheer.

The markets have also inspired similar celebrations around the world, from France to New York, but Strasbourg remains the heart of this particular style of celebration. The city's commitment to maintaining the authenticity and charm of its Christmas markets has ensured that they remain a beloved tradition for both locals and visitors alike.

Why Visit Strasbourg Christmas Markets??

 ## Historical Significance:

Strasbourg's Christmas markets, known as the Christkindelsmärik, are among the oldest in Europe, dating back to 1570. This rich history adds a layer of depth and tradition to your visit, making it more than just a shopping trip but a journey through time.

 ## Festive Atmosphere:

Strasbourg is often referred to as the "Capital of Christmas," and for good reason. The entire city is adorned with twinkling lights, festive decorations, and charming wooden chalets. The atmosphere is filled with the joyous sounds of carolers, the delightful aroma of spiced wine, and the cheerful chatter of visitors from around the world.

 ## Unique Shopping Experience:

The markets have a lot of handmade items, including detailed ornaments, decorations, unique gifts, and souvenirs. These products are not only beautiful but also reflect the skilled craft of Alsace. They make wonderful holiday gifts that are special and unforgettable.

 ## Culinary Delights:

Food lovers will be in heaven at the Strasbourg Christmas markets. The stalls are brimming with traditional Alsatian treats such as bredele (Christmas cookies), flammekueche (a type of flatbread), and choucroute (sauerkraut with sausages).

Don't miss out on the vin chaud (mulled wine), which is perfect for warming up on a chilly winter evening.

Stunning Architecture:

Strasbourg's architecture is a blend of French and German influences, and during the Christmas season, it becomes even more magical. The Strasbourg Cathedral, with its towering Gothic spires, is a must-see. The light displays on the cathedral and other historic buildings create a breathtaking backdrop for the markets.

Cultural Immersion:

Visiting the Strasbourg Christmas markets is an opportunity to immerse yourself in local traditions and customs. From the nativity scenes to the festive music and performances, you'll get a taste of Alsatian culture and the true spirit of Christmas.

Family-Friendly Activities:

The markets are perfect for families, with plenty of activities to keep children entertained. From merry-go-rounds and ice skating rinks to storytelling sessions and craft workshops, there's something for everyone to enjoy.

Scenic Beauty:

Strasbourg is a picturesque city, and during the Christmas season, it transforms into a fairy tale setting. The cobblestone streets, half-timbered houses, and the gentle flow of the river Ill all contribute to the city's enchanting ambiance.

Accessibility:

Strasbourg is easily accessible by train, car, or plane, making it a convenient destination for travelers. The city's well-organized public transport system also makes it easy to navigate and explore all the different markets and attractions.

Memorable Experiences:

Above all, visiting the Strasbourg Christmas markets is about creating unforgettable memories. Whether you're sipping hot chocolate while watching the snow fall, finding the perfect gift for a loved one, or simply soaking in the festive spirit, your visit to Strasbourg will be a cherished experience that you'll remember for years to come.

Christmas Customs And Traditions In Strasbourg

The Great Christmas Tree

A central symbol of Strasbourg's Christmas celebrations is the Great Christmas Tree at Place Kléber. Standing at around 30 meters tall, this majestic tree is beautifully decorated and illuminated, creating a stunning focal point for the city's festive activities. The tradition of the Christmas tree in Alsace dates back to the 16th century, making it one of the earliest regions to adopt this custom.

Advent Wreaths

The Advent wreath is a significant tradition in Strasbourg, originating from Protestant Germany in the 1830s. The wreath, made of evergreen branches and adorned with four candles, symbolizes the four weeks of Advent. Each Sunday leading up to Christmas, a new candle is lit, representing the anticipation of the coming of Christ. This tradition is widely observed in Alsatian homes and churches.

Saint Nicholas and Hans Trapp

Saint Nicholas, celebrated on December 6th, is a key figure in Alsatian Christmas traditions. He is known for bringing gifts to children, similar to Santa Claus. Accompanying him is Hans Trapp, a folklore character who is said to punish naughty children. This duality of reward and punishment is a unique aspect of the region's festive customs.

Christmas Lights and Decorations

Strasbourg is famous for its stunning Christmas lights and decorations. The city's streets, squares, and buildings are adorned with twinkling lights, creating a magical ambiance. Key areas like Rue des Orfèvres and Rue Mercière are particularly known for their elaborate light displays. The illumination of the city is a highlight of the festive season, drawing visitors from around the world.

Christmas Concerts and Performances

Music plays a significant role in Strasbourg's Christmas celebrations. The Strasbourg Cathedral and other venues host a variety of concerts featuring classical, choral, and festive music.

These performances add to the spiritual and cultural richness of the season, providing moments of reflection and joy.

The Christmas Lantern

The Christmas lantern is another charming tradition in Strasbourg. These lanterns, often handcrafted, are used to decorate homes and public spaces, adding a warm and festive glow to the city. The lanterns symbolize light and hope, enhancing the magical atmosphere of the season.

The Walk To The Stars

The "Walk to the Stars" is a unique and enchanting experience where visitors follow a trail of illuminated stars through the city. This guided walk takes participants through some of Strasbourg's most beautiful and festive areas, providing a magical way to explore the city and its Christmas traditions.

CHAPTER 2

Best Time To Visit?

Choosing the best time to visit Strasbourg Christmas Markets depends on your preferences and what you want to experience. Here are some suggestions for the best times to visit:

Early December

Visiting in early December offers a perfect balance between festive cheer and manageable crowds. The markets are fully set up, and the city is beautifully decorated, but it's not as crowded as it gets closer to Christmas. This is an ideal time for those who want to enjoy the markets at a leisurely pace, take in the sights, and shop without the hustle and bustle of peak season.

Weekdays vs. Weekends

Weekdays are generally less crowded than weekends. If you can, plan your visit from Monday to Thursday to avoid the weekend rush. This will give you more space to explore the stalls, enjoy the food, and take in the festive atmosphere without feeling overwhelmed by the crowds.

Late Afternoon to Early Evening

The best time of day to visit the markets is late afternoon to early evening. This is when the lights start to twinkle, creating a magical ambiance. The markets are typically busiest after sunset, so arriving a bit earlier allows you to enjoy the transition from day to night.

You can shop for souvenirs and gifts during the day and return in the evening to admire the beautiful illuminations and enjoy a cup of mulled wine.

 ## Special Events And Activities

Strasbourg's Christmas markets are not just about shopping; they also feature a variety of special events and activities. Check the market's schedule for concerts, parades, and other festive events. Attending these can add an extra layer of enjoyment to your visit. The weekends often have more events, but they also attract larger crowds.

 ## Avoiding Peak Times

The markets are busiest in the days leading up to Christmas. If you prefer a quieter experience, try to avoid visiting from December 20th to 24th. This period sees a significant influx of visitors, making it harder to navigate the markets and enjoy the stalls. If you must visit during this time, going early in the day can help you avoid the worst of the crowds.

 ## Post-Christmas

While the main markets close on December 24th, some smaller markets and festive activities continue until the end of the year. Visiting after Christmas can be a more relaxed experience, with fewer crowds and a more laid-back atmosphere. It's a great time to enjoy the city's decorations and festive spirit without the rush of pre-Christmas shopping.

Tips for Planning Your Visit?

 Book Accommodation Early:

Strasbourg is a popular destination during the festive season, so it's essential to book your accommodation well in advance. Consider staying in the city center to be close to the main markets and attractions. Hotels, B&Bs, and vacation rentals are all good options. Some recommended areas include Petite France and around the Strasbourg Cathedral.

 Dress Warmly:

December in Strasbourg can be quite cold, with temperatures often around freezing. Dress in layers to stay warm, and don't forget essentials like a hat, gloves, scarf, and warm socks. Comfortable, waterproof footwear is also a must, as you'll be spending a lot of time walking around.

 Explore Different Markets:

Strasbourg boasts several Christmas markets, each with its unique charm. The main market at Place Broglie is the oldest and most famous. Other notable markets include Place Kléber, known for its giant Christmas tree, and Place de la Cathédrale, which offers a magical atmosphere with the stunning Strasbourg Cathedral as a backdrop. Make sure to visit multiple markets to get a full experience.

Try Local Delicacies:

Food is a highlight of the Strasbourg Christmas markets. Be sure to try traditional Alsatian treats such as bredele (Christmas cookies), flammekueche (a type of flatbread), and choucroute (sauerkraut with sausages). Warm up with a cup of vin chaud (mulled wine) or hot chocolate as you explore the stalls.

 ## Attend Special Events:

Check the market's schedule for special events such as concerts, parades, and light shows. These events add an extra layer of festivity to your visit. The light show at the Strasbourg Cathedral and the daily lighting of the Christmas tree at Place Kléber is particularly popular.

 ## Shop for Unique Gifts:

The markets are a treasure trove of handcrafted goods, from ornaments and decorations to unique gifts and souvenirs. Look for items that are unique to the region, such as handmade pottery, wooden toys, and local delicacies. These make for perfect holiday gifts that are both meaningful and memorable.

 ## Use Public Transport:

Strasbourg has an excellent public transport system, including trams and buses, which makes it easy to get around the city. Consider purchasing a Strasbourg Pass, which offers unlimited travel on public transport and discounts on various attractions. If you're driving, be aware that parking can be challenging during the festive season, so using public transport is often more convenient.

Stay Safe and Healthy:

With large crowds and cold weather, it's crucial to stay safe and healthy. Watch your belongings, especially in crowded areas. Stay hydrated and take breaks to warm up indoors. If you're traveling with children, make sure they are dressed warmly and keep a close eye on them in the busy markets.

How To Get There??

 By Air

Strasbourg Airport (SXB) is the closest airport to the city, located about 10 kilometers southwest of Strasbourg. It offers both domestic and international flights. From the airport, you can take a shuttle train to the city center, which takes around 10 minutes.

For more international options, you can fly to Basel-Mulhouse-Freiburg Airport (BSL/MLH/EAP), which is about 130 kilometers away. From there, you can take a train or rent a car to reach Strasbourg.

 By Train

Strasbourg is well-served by the French high-speed train network, the TGV. The Strasbourg-Ville Train Station is centrally located and offers direct connections to major cities in France and neighboring countries.

> • *FROM PARIS: The TGV from Paris to Strasbourg*
> *takes approximately 1 hour and 46 minutes*

- *FROM FRANKFURT: Direct trains from Frankfurt to Strasbourg take about 2 hours.*

- *FROM BASEL: The journey from Basel to Strasbourg by train takes around 1 hour and 20 minutes.*

🚗 By Car

Driving to Strasbourg can be a scenic and flexible option, especially if you plan to explore the surrounding Alsace region. The city is easily accessible through major highways:

- *FROM PARIS: The drive takes about 5 hours via the A4 motorway.*

- *FROM FRANKFURT: The drive takes around 2.5 hours via the A5 motorway.*

- *FROM BASEL: The drive takes about 1.5 hours via the A35 motorway*

NOTE: Parking can be challenging during the festive season, so consider using park-and-ride facilities on the outskirts of the city and taking public transport into the center.

🚌 By Bus

Several bus companies offer routes to Strasbourg from various European cities. This can be a cost-effective option, though travel times are generally longer than by train or car.

FlixBus and Eurolines are popular choices, with routes connecting Strasbourg to cities like Paris, Brussels, and Munich.

How To Get Around The Christmas Markets??

 ## Walking

Strasbourg is a pedestrian-friendly city, and many of the Christmas markets are within walking distance of each other. Walking allows you to fully immerse yourself in the festive atmosphere, discover hidden gems, and enjoy the beautiful decorations and lights along the way. The main markets, such as those at Place Broglie, Place de la Cathédrale, and Place Kléber, are all centrally located and easily accessible on foot.

 ## Public Transport

Strasbourg has an efficient public transport system operated by the CTS (Compagnie des Transports Strasbourgeois), which includes trams and buses. Here's how you can use them to get around:

> • *TRAMS: The tram network is extensive and covers most of the city, including key areas where the Christmas markets are located. Lines A, B, C, D, and F are particularly useful for reaching the markets. For example, Line A and D can take you to the Homme de Fer station, which is close to several markets.*

> • *BUSES: Buses complement the tram network and can take you to areas not covered by trams. They are a good option if you're staying in a more residential area or need to reach a specific market.*

NOTE: Consider purchasing a Strasbourg Pass, which offers unlimited travel on public transport and discounts on various attractions.

Cycling

Strasbourg is known for being a bike-friendly city with an extensive network of bike paths. You can rent a bike from various rental shops or use the city's bike-sharing system, Vélhop. Cycling is a great way to cover more ground quickly while still enjoying the festive atmosphere. Just be sure to dress warmly and follow local cycling rules.

Taxis And Ride Sharing

Taxis and ride-sharing services like Uber are available in Strasbourg and can be a convenient option if you're traveling with a lot of shopping bags or prefer a more direct route to your destination. However, they can be more expensive than public transport, especially during peak times.

Hop-On Hop-Off Tours

For a more structured way to explore the markets, consider joining a hop-on hop-off tour. These tours typically include stops at major markets and attractions, allowing you to explore at your own pace while providing convenient transportation between locations. This can be especially useful if you're short on time or prefer a guided experience.

Best Places To Stay Near Strasbourg Christmas Markets

---

1. Grand Île (Old Town)

The Grand Île, Strasbourg's historic center, is a UNESCO World Heritage site and the heart of the city's Christmas festivities. Staying here puts you within walking distance of major markets and attractions.

Accommodations In Grand Île

Maison Rouge Strasbourg Hotel & Spa, Autograph Collection

The Maison Rouge Strasbourg Hotel is a historic establishment located in the heart of Strasbourg, near Place Kléber. This hotel is known for its elegant Art Deco style and modern amenities. It offers 131 rooms and suites, some with views of the Strasbourg Cathedral. You can enjoy the on-site restaurant, "Le 1387," which serves gourmet meals, and the Salons Mistinguett for breakfast and brunch. The hotel also features a spa with a hammam, sauna, whirlpool bath, and sensory shower, providing a luxurious retreat after a day exploring the Christmas markets.

DETAILS:

Address: *4, rue des Francs-Bourgeois, 67000 Strasbourg*

No of Rooms: *131 Rooms*

Contact Line: *+33388320860*

Email: *info@maison-rouge.com*

Hotel Gutenberg

Hôtel Gutenberg is a highly-rated hotel close to the Strasbourg Cathedral. It provides cozy rooms equipped with modern facilities like free Wi-Fi and satellite TV. The hotel is famous for its welcoming staff and prime location, making it an ideal choice for those wanting to visit the Christmas markets and the historic center of Strasbourg.

DETAILS:

Address: 31 Rue des Serruriers, 67000 Strasbourg

No of Rooms: 42 Rooms

Contact Line: +33 3 88 32 17 15

Email: info@hotel-gutenberg.com

Hotel Suisse

Hotel Suisse is a charming boutique hotel situated at the foot of the Strasbourg Cathedral. This hotel offers 25 uniquely decorated rooms, many with views of the cathedral. The hotel's Alsatian "Stub" provides a cozy setting for a gourmet buffet breakfast, featuring local specialties like Kougelhof. The Café Suisse, open throughout the day, is perfect for a relaxing break.

DETAILS:

Address: 2/4 Rue de la Râpe, Strasbourg, 67000

No of Rooms: 25 Rooms

Contact Line: +33 3 88 35 22 11

Email: info@hotel-suisse.com

2. La Petite France

La Petite France is a picturesque district known for its half-timbered houses and cobblestone streets. It's a short walk from the main Christmas markets and offers a romantic setting.

Accommodations In La Petite France

Hôtel & Spa Régent Petite France

Hôtel & Spa Régent Petite France is a 5-star hotel located in the heart of the Petite France district. Set in a historic building, this hotel offers luxurious rooms with stunning views of the canals. The hotel features a spa with a range of treatments, a fitness center, and a gourmet restaurant. Its prime location provides easy access to the Christmas markets and other key attractions in Strasbourg.

DETAILS:

Address: 5 rue des Moulins 67000 Strasbourg

No of Rooms: 75 Rooms

Contact Line: +33 3 88 76 43 43

Email: accueil@regent-petite-france.com

Hotel Le Bouclier d'Or

Le Bouclier D'or is a 4-star hotel located in a 16th-century building in the Petite France district. This hotel combines historic charm with modern luxury. The rooms and suites are elegantly decorated, and the hotel features a wine bar and a wellness center with a spa, sauna, hammam, and massage services.

Address: *1 Rue du Bouclier, 67000 Strasbourg*

No of Rooms: *22 Rooms*

Contact Line: *+33 3 88 13 73 55*

Email: *contact@lebouclierdor.com*

Hotel Les Haras

Hotel Les Haras is a luxurious 4-star hotel set in a historic 18th-century building. Located at the entrance to the Petite France district, this hotel offers a blend of historic charm and modern comfort. The rooms are elegantly decorated with contemporary furniture and high-quality materials. The hotel features a spa with a hammam, sauna, and indoor pool, as well as a fitness center. You can also enjoy dining at the on-site brasserie, which offers a gourmet menu.

DETAILS:

Address: *23 Glacier Street, 67000 Strasbourg*

No of Rooms: *115 Rooms*

Contact Line: *+33 3 90 20 50 00*

Email: *info@les-haras-hotel.com*

3. Neustadt

Neustadt, the "new town," is known for its grand boulevards and 19th-century architecture. It's a bit quieter than the city center but still within easy reach of the Christmas markets.

Accommodations In Neustadt

Hotel D Strasbourg

Hotel D Strasbourg is a 4-star design hotel located in the heart of Neustadt, just a short walk from the Strasbourg Cathedral and the Christmas markets. The hotel offers modern and elegantly decorated rooms equipped with the latest technology, including flat-screen TVs, iPod docks, and free Wi-Fi. You can enjoy a fitness center, sauna, and a relaxation room with heated loungers. The hotel also provides a daily breakfast featuring organic and local products.

DETAILS:

Address: 15, Rue du Fossé des 13, 67000, Strasbourg

No of Rooms: 37 Rooms

Contact Line: +33 3 88 15 13 67

Email: sleep@hoteld.fr

Le Moon

Le Moon is a boutique hotel known for its stylish and contemporary design. Located in Neustadt, it offers a unique blend of comfort and luxury. The hotel features spacious rooms with modern amenities, including free Wi-Fi, flat-screen TVs, and minibars. You can enjoy a cozy lounge area and a bar serving a variety of drinks.

DETAILS:

Address: 4 Quai Jacques-Sturm, 67000, Strasbourg

No of Rooms: 10 Rooms

Contact Line: +33 7 69 65 63 96

Hotel Regent Contades

Hotel Regent Contades is a 4-star hotel situated along the Ill River in Neustadt. This historic hotel offers elegant rooms with classic decor and modern amenities, including free Wi-Fi, flat-screen TVs, and minibars. The hotel features a wellness area with a sauna and a hammam, as well as a bar and lounge for relaxing after a day of sightseeing.

DETAILS:

Address: 8 Avenue de la Liberté, Strasbourg, 67000

No of Rooms: 48 Rooms

Contact Line: +33 3 88 15 05 05

Email: info@regent-contades.com

4. Krutenau

Krutenau is a lively neighborhood with a bohemian vibe, known for its cafes, bars, and boutiques. It's a short walk from the city center and the Christmas markets.

Accommodations In Krutenau

Hotel Beaucour

Hotel Beaucour is a charming boutique hotel located in the lively Krutenau district. The hotel offers individually decorated rooms with a cozy and welcoming atmosphere. Each room is equipped with modern amenities, including free Wi-Fi, flat-screen TVs, and minibars. The hotel features a beautiful courtyard and a breakfast room where you can enjoy a buffet breakfast with local specialties.

Address: 5 Rue des Bouchers, 67000, Strasbourg

No of Rooms: 49 Rooms

Contact Line: +33 3 88 76 72 00

Email: info@hotel-beaucour.com

Hotel Cour du Corbeau Strasbourg - MGallery

Hotel Cour du Corbeau Strasbourg - MGallery is a luxurious 4-star hotel set in a beautifully restored 16th-century building in Krutenau. The hotel offers elegant rooms and suites with a blend of historic charm and modern comfort. Each room is equipped with flat-screen TVs, free Wi-Fi, and minibars. The hotel features a bar, a terrace, and a breakfast room where you can enjoy a gourmet breakfast.

DETAILS:

Address: 6-8 rue des Couples, 67000, Strasbourg

No of Rooms: 63 Rooms

Contact Line: +33390002626

Email: H7575@accor.com

5. Quartier de la Gare

Quartier de la Gare is the area surrounding the Strasbourg train station (Gare de Strasbourg). This district is known for its convenient location and excellent transport links, making it an ideal base for visitors arriving by train.

Accommodations In Quartier de la Gare

Hôtel Tandem

Hôtel Tandem is a boutique hotel situated very close to the Strasbourg train station. This environmentally friendly hotel features modern, stylish rooms with sustainable design touches. Every room includes free Wi-Fi, flat-screen TVs, and minibars. The hotel features a cozy lounge area, a bar, and a breakfast room where you can enjoy a buffet breakfast with organic and local products.

DETAILS:

Address: *2 Place De La Gare, 67000, Strasbourg*

No of Rooms: *70 Rooms*

Contact Line: *+33 3 88 22 30 30*

Email: *reservations@hotel-tandem.fr*

Best Western Plus Monopole

Best Western Plus Monopole Métropole is a 4-star hotel located near the Strasbourg train station. It provides comfortable, well-furnished rooms equipped with modern amenities such as free Wi-Fi, flat-screen TVs, and minibars. You can enjoy a fitness center, a bar, and a breakfast room where a buffet breakfast is served daily.

DETAILS:

Address: *16, rue Kuhn - 67000, Strasbourg*

No of Rooms: *81 rooms*

Contact Line: *+33 3 88 14 39 14*

Email: *infos@bw-monopole.com*

CHAPTER 3

Exploring Strasbourg Christmas Markets

Opening Dates

The Strasbourg Christmas markets typically open from late November to Christmas Eve. For 2024, the markets are scheduled to run from November 27th to December 27th.

Chrìstkìndelsmärik at Place Broglie

The Chrìstkìndelsmärik at Place Broglie is one of the oldest Christmas markets in Europe. It began in 1570 and was initially held in various parts of Strasbourg, including Place Kléber and Place du Château. However, it eventually settled at Place Broglie in 1871.

This festive market boasts over 100 stalls and is the largest Christmas market in Strasbourg. You can explore a variety of items, including decorations, pottery, glass jewelry, and handmade toys. It's an ideal spot to shop for Christmas decorations to adorn your home.
And don't forget to capture a memorable photo under the Chrìstkìndelsmärik arch during your time in Strasbourg.

Address: *Place Broglie, 67000 Strasbourg, France*

Place Kléber Christmas Market

Place Kléber, located in the heart of the Grande Île, is home to the Grand Sapin, which is Strasbourg's iconic Christmas tree. Provided annually by France's National Forestry Office, this majestic tree stands at least 30 meters (98 feet) tall. The search for the perfect tree starts early each year, usually in March. To achieve its glamorous shape, they even add more branches from other trees. Once adorned, the tree dazzles with 7 kilometers of twinkling lights, baubles, angels, and stars —truly one of the most sumptuous Christmas trees you'll ever see.

Don't miss the musical illuminations, which occur every hour on the hour between 4 PM and 9 PM.

In the past, people used to place presents for the poor under the Christmas tree. Nowadays, at the foot of the Grand Sapin, you'll find the Village du Partage (Village of Sharing). Here, nearly 90 charities operate across 14 stalls, selling souvenirs and food for a good cause. And if you're craving traditional Alsatian and French delicacies, you're in luck—sausages, bretzels, flammkuchen, crepes, and mulled wine await.

Address: *Place Kléber, 67000 Strasbourg, France*

Place de la Cathédrale Christmas Markets

At the base of the Strasbourg Cathedral, which used to host the Klausenmärik (St. Nicholas Market) in the Middle Ages, there are historic stalls selling gingerbread, Bredele, Christmas decorations, and more. These stalls at Place de la Cathédrale have expanded over time to Place du Château, Rue des Hallebardes, and Rue Gutenberg.

When you're near the cathedral, visit the first floor of Le 5e Lieu for excellent views of the market and a free permanent exhibition about Strasbourg's history. During the holidays, don't miss the 60-foot-long nativity scene inside the cathedral, dating back to 1907, which you can see for free.

Address: Place de la Cathédrale & Place du Château, 67000 Strasbourg, France

The Quai des Délices Christmas Markets

As the name implies, the Quai des Délices markets are a dream spot for anyone who loves food. The terrace at the Palais Rohan offers the ideal setting to sample local Alsatian wines during the Strasbourg Christmas market, whereas beer lovers might prefer the nearby Place du Marché-aux-Poissons. At night, this area is fantastic for watching boats on the River Ill and admiring the nearly 400 stars hanging between the Pont du Corbeau and Pont Saint-Guillaume.

Address: Place du Marché-des-Poissons & The terrace of the Palais Rohan, 67000 Strasbourg, France

Carré d'Or Christmas Market

Just a short walk from the Cathedral, you'll know you've reached the Carré d'Or, or the old Gold Quarter, as the streets turn into a magical winter scene. This area, which used to be home to goldsmiths, now has many shops and restaurants that go all out for the holidays.

The market at Place du Temple Neuf is packed with candles, jewelry, and delicious food.

After checking out the market stalls, take a stroll through the beautifully decorated streets. You'll see a lot of lights and shop windows filled with stuffed animals, ornaments, holly, branches, and more. It's a must-see when you visit Strasbourg in the winter.

Address: *Place du Temple-Neuf, 67000 Strasbourg, France*

La Petite Christmas Markets

La Petite France is one of the most picturesque areas in Strasbourg, and it becomes even more enchanting during Christmas. This historic part of the city hosts two Christmas markets, located at Place Benjamin Zix and Place Saint-Thomas. Here, you can find stalls selling candles and Christmas decorations, as well as hot beverages and a variety of sweet and savory treats. Don't forget to take a photo at the canal lock near Place Benjamin Zix.

Address: *Place Benjamin Zix & Place Saint-Thomas,*
67000 Strasbourg, France

Advent Village At Square Louise-Weiss

The Advent Village at Louise Weiss Square in Petite France comes alive in December. Thousands of lights beautifully illuminate the area, creating a magical setting for strolling.

Local farmers and artisans, known as the Irréductibles Petits Producteurs d'Alsace, offer a delightful array of local products from the Alsace region—think jams, chocolate, and bio wines. You can also join workshops to explore Alsatian Christmas traditions or enjoy frequent concerts.

Address: Square Louise-Weiss, 67000 Strasbourg, France

Off Market At Place Grimmeissen

The OFF Christmas market at Place Grimmeissen is one of Strasbourg's more unique markets, focused on sustainability and community. It's a fantastic spot to find Christmas gifts made from recycled materials or ethically sourced items. Here, you can also barter or trade for gifts, making it a special sharing market.

Address: Place Grimmeissen, 67000 Strasbourg, France

CHAPTER 4

Best Events & Things To Do In Strasbourg During Christmas

Christmas Concerts And Events

1. Christmas Concerts at Strasbourg Cathedral

The Strasbourg Cathedral, a stunning Gothic masterpiece, hosts several Christmas concerts throughout the festive season. These concerts often feature classical and choral music, creating a serene and uplifting atmosphere. The cathedral's magnificent acoustics and beautiful decorations make these performances a truly magical experience.

2. Concerts at St. Thomas Church

St. Thomas Church, another historic landmark in Strasbourg, offers a series of Advent and Christmas concerts. Known for its impressive Silbermann organ, the church hosts performances that include:

- *ORGAN RECITALS: Showcasing the church's historic organ, these recitals feature works by composers such as Bach and Handel.*

- *CHORAL CONCERTS: Featuring local and visiting choirs, these concerts present a mix of sacred and festive music.*

3. Opéra National du Rhin

The Opéra National du Rhin in Strasbourg presents a variety of performances during the Christmas season, including operas, ballets, and concerts. The opera house, located at Place Broglie, is a beautiful venue that adds a touch of elegance to any performance. Special Christmas-themed shows and events often include:

- *CHRISTMAS GALA CONCERTS: Featuring a mix of opera arias, orchestral pieces, and festive music.*

- *BALLET PERFORMANCES: Classic ballets such as "The Nutcracker" are often part of the holiday program.*

4. Palais de la Musique et des Congrès

The Palais de la Musique et des Congrès is a major cultural venue in Strasbourg that hosts a wide range of events, including concerts, theater performances, and exhibitions. During the Christmas season, you can expect a variety of festive concerts and shows, featuring everything from classical music to contemporary performances. Highlights include:

- *SYMPHONY CONCERTS: Performed by the Strasbourg Philharmonic Orchestra, these concerts often feature works by composers such as Beethoven, Mozart, and Tchaikovsky.*

- *CHRISTMAS SPECIALS: Concerts featuring festive music, carols, and popular Christmas songs.*

5. La Maison Bleue

La Maison Bleue is a cultural venue in Strasbourg that hosts a variety of events, including concerts, exhibitions, and workshops. During the Christmas season, you can find special festive events and performances, adding to the city's rich cultural offerings. Highlights include:

• JAZZ AND CONTEMPORARY MUSIC: Featuring local and international artists, these concerts offer a modern twist to the festive celebrations.

• FAMILY CONCERTS: Designed for all ages, these concerts often include interactive elements and festive themes.

6. Christmas Eve and New Year's Eve Celebrations

Strasbourg hosts special events on Christmas Eve and New Year's Eve, including festive dinners, parties, and fireworks displays. Many restaurants and hotels offer special holiday menus and entertainment, making these evenings particularly memorable.

7. Ososphère Festival

The Ososphère Festival is a contemporary arts festival held in Strasbourg, featuring a mix of music, visual arts, and digital culture. While it typically takes place in the spring, the festival often hosts special events and performances during the Christmas season, adding a modern twist to the festive celebrations.

8. Planetarium Shows

The Strasbourg Planetarium offers special shows during the Christmas season, including presentations on the starry skies around Christmas. These shows provide a fascinating and educational experience for visitors of all ages.

9. The Great Christmas Tree Lighting Ceremony

The lighting of the Great Christmas Tree at Place Kléber is a highlight of the festive season. Standing at around 30 meters tall, this majestic tree is beautifully decorated and illuminated, creating a stunning focal point for the city's celebrations. The lighting ceremony is accompanied by music and other festive activities, making it a must-see event.

Other Best Things To Do In Strasbourg During Christmas

1. Admire the Strasbourg Cathedral

The Strasbourg Cathedral, or Cathédrale Notre-Dame de Strasbourg, is a must-visit landmark. During Christmas, the cathedral is beautifully illuminated and often hosts special concerts and events. Climb to the top for a panoramic view of the city and its festive lights.

2. Explore La Petite France

La Petite France is a picturesque district with charming half-timbered houses and cobblestone streets. During Christmas, this area is adorned with festive decorations and lights, creating a magical atmosphere. Take a stroll or enjoy a boat tour along the canals to fully appreciate the beauty of this historic neighborhood.

3. Visit the Palais Rohan

The Palais Rohan is a grand palace that houses three museums: the Museum of Fine Arts, the Archaeological Museum, and the Museum of Decorative Arts. During the Christmas season, the palace often hosts special exhibitions and events. It's a great place to immerse yourself in art and history while enjoying the festive ambiance.

4. Enjoy the Festive Lights

Strasbourg is renowned for its stunning Christmas lights. Key areas to explore include:

- *RUE DES ORFÈVRES: Famous for its beautiful light displays and festive decorations.*

- *RUE MERCIÈRE: Offers a magical view of the Strasbourg Cathedral with twinkling lights.*

- *PLACE GUTENBERG: Features unique light displays and a small Christmas market.*

5. Take a Day Trip To Neighboring Towns

Strasbourg's location in the Alsace region makes it an ideal base for exploring nearby towns, which also host charming Christmas markets. Consider visiting:

- *COLMAR: Known for its fairy-tale architecture and multiple Christmas markets.*

- *OBERNAI: A quaint town with a lively Christmas market and festive activities.*

6. Visit the Alsatian Museum

The Alsatian Museum offers a fascinating insight into the region's culture and traditions. During Christmas, the museum often hosts special exhibitions and events related to Alsatian holiday customs, making it a great place to learn more about the local heritage.

7. Ice Skating at Place Dauphine

For a fun and festive activity, head to the ice skating rink at Place Dauphine. Whether you're an experienced skater or a beginner, gliding on the ice surrounded by festive decorations is a delightful experience for all ages.

8. Discover the Caves Historiques des Hospices

The Caves Historiques des Hospices is an underground wine cellar dating back to the 14th century. It offers a unique opportunity to taste and purchase local wines, including some rare vintages. The cellar is beautifully decorated for Christmas, adding to the festive experience.

9. Visit the Musée de l'Œuvre Notre-Dame

This museum, located near the Strasbourg Cathedral, houses a collection of medieval and Renaissance art from the Upper Rhine region. During Christmas, the museum often features special exhibitions and events related to the festive season.

CHAPTER 5

Must Try Foods & Drinks At The Strasbourg Christmas Markets

 Bredle

Bredle are traditional Alsatian Christmas cookies that come in a variety of flavors and shapes. These delightful treats are a staple during the festive season. Popular varieties include Butterbredle (butter cookies), Schwowebredle (almond and cinnamon cookies), and Anisbredle (aniseed cookies). They are perfect for snacking as you wander through the markets or as a sweet souvenir to take home.

 Flammekueche (Tarte Flambée)

Flammekueche, also known as tarte flambée, is a thin, crispy flatbread topped with crème fraîche, onions, and lardons (bacon). It's a savory delight that is often compared to pizza but with a distinct Alsatian twist. Variations include toppings like mushrooms, Munster cheese, or even salmon, making it a versatile and delicious option.

 Choucroute Garnie

Choucroute garnie is a hearty dish of sauerkraut cooked with white wine and served with an assortment of meats, including sausages, pork knuckles, and bacon. This traditional Alsatian dish is perfect for warming up on a cold winter day and is a must-try for meat lovers.

 Foie Gras

Alsace is renowned for its foie gras, and the Christmas markets are an excellent place to sample this luxurious delicacy. Typically served as a pâté or terrine, foie gras is rich, buttery, and a true gourmet experience. Look for stalls offering locally produced foie gras for the best quality.

Pretzels

Pretzels are a beloved snack in Alsace, and you'll find them in abundance at the Christmas markets. These soft, doughy treats are often sprinkled with coarse salt and can be enjoyed plain or with various toppings like cheese or mustard. They are perfect for a quick, satisfying snack as you explore the markets.

Spaetzle

Spaetzle are small, soft egg noodles that are a traditional side dish in Alsatian cuisine. At the Christmas markets, you can find spaetzle served in various ways, such as with cheese (similar to mac and cheese), with mushrooms, or even with sauerkraut and bacon. It's a comforting and filling dish that pairs well with many of the market's other offerings.

Maennele

Maennele are sweet, brioche-like buns shaped like little men, traditionally enjoyed on Saint Nicholas Day. These charming treats are often decorated with raisins or chocolate chips for eyes and are a delightful snack for both children and adults.

Christstollen

Christstollen is a festive bread made with dried fruits, nuts, and spices, generously dusted with powdered sugar. This rich, dense cake is perfect for breakfast or as a snack with a cup of coffee or tea. It also keeps well, making it a great treat to bring home.

 # Gingerbread (Lebkuchen)

Gingerbread is a quintessential Christmas treat, and the Strasbourg markets offer a variety of gingerbread delights. From intricately decorated cookies to soft, spiced cakes, gingerbread is a must-try. The subtle honey and spice flavors make it a perfect festive snack.

 # Vin Chaud (Mulled Wine)

No visit to the Strasbourg Christmas markets is complete without a cup of vin chaud. This warm, spiced wine is made with red or white wine, mixed with spices, sugar, and citrus fruits. It's the perfect drink to warm you up as you stroll through the markets, enjoying the festive atmosphere.

 # Christmas Beer

Alsace is known for its beer, and during the festive season, many local breweries produce special Christmas beers. These brews are typically more robust and spiced, with notes of citrus and honey. Sampling a Christmas beer is a great way to experience the local brewing tradition.

 Dampfnudel

Dampfnudel are soft, steamed buns that are often served with a sweet or savory filling. At the Christmas markets, you might find them served with fruit compote or a creamy sauce, making for a comforting and satisfying treat.

International Cuisines At The Strasbourg Christmas Markets

German Specialties

• BRATWURST: These delicious German sausages are often grilled and served in a bun with mustard or sauerkraut.

• PRETZELS: Soft, doughy pretzels sprinkled with coarse salt are a popular snack, perfect for munching on as you explore the markets.

• LEBKUCHEN: Traditional German gingerbread cookies, often decorated with icing and nuts, are a festive treat.

Swiss Delicacies

• RACLETTE: Melted Swiss cheese served over potatoes, pickles, and onions is a comforting and indulgent dish.

• FONDUE: Warm, gooey cheese fondue is perfect for dipping bread and vegetables, offering a cozy and communal eating experience.

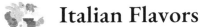 Italian Flavors

• PIZZA: Wood-fired pizzas with a variety of toppings are a popular choice for a quick and satisfying meal.

• PANETTONE: This sweet, fluffy Italian bread studded with dried fruits and nuts is a holiday favorite.

Spanish Tapas

• CHURROS: These deep-fried dough pastries, often dusted with sugar and served with a side of chocolate sauce, are a sweet treat.

• PAELLA: A hearty dish of saffron-infused rice cooked with seafood, chicken, and vegetables, paella is a flavorful and filling option.

Middle Eastern Cuisine

• FALAFEL: These deep-fried chickpea balls are often served in pita bread with fresh vegetables and tahini sauce.

• BAKLAVA: A dessert pastry made from layers of filo dough, stuffed with chopped nuts, and sweetened with honey or syrup.

Asian Influences

• SUSHI: Freshly made sushi rolls offer a light and healthy option amid the rich festive foods.

• NOODLES: Stir-fried noodles with vegetables, meat, or tofu provide a quick and tasty meal.

American Classics

• BURGERS: Gourmet burgers with a variety of toppings are a popular choice.

• HOT DOGS: Classic hot dogs with mustard, ketchup, and relish are a convenient and satisfying snack.

African and Caribbean Flavors

• JOLLOF RICE: A flavorful West African dish made with rice, tomatoes, and spices.

• JERK CHICKEN: Spicy and aromatic, this Caribbean favorite is often grilled and served with rice and peas.

CHAPTER 6

Shopping At Strasbourg Christmas Markets

Best Things To Buy At The Strasbourg Christmas Market?

 ### Handcrafted Ornaments

One of the most popular items at the Strasbourg Christmas markets are the handcrafted ornaments. These beautiful decorations come in a variety of styles, from traditional wooden figures to intricately painted glass baubles. Many of these ornaments are made by local artisans, ensuring that each piece is unique and of high quality. They make perfect gifts or additions to your own Christmas tree.

 ### Alsatian Pottery

Alsatian pottery is known for its distinctive blue and white designs, often featuring floral or geometric patterns. At the markets, you can find a range of pottery items, including bowls, plates, mugs, and decorative pieces. These handcrafted items are not only beautiful but also functional, making them great souvenirs or gifts.

Wooden Toys

For a touch of nostalgia, consider purchasing traditional wooden toys. These charming items are often handmade and painted, reflecting the craftsmanship and attention to detail of the artisans. From toy trains and puzzles to dolls and figurines, wooden toys are perfect for children and collectors alike.

 # Christmas Cookies (Bredle)

Bredle are traditional Alsatian Christmas cookies that come in a variety of flavors and shapes. These delicious treats are a staple of the holiday season and make for great gifts or snacks to enjoy while exploring the markets. Popular varieties include butter cookies, almond cookies, and aniseed cookies.

 # Local Wines and Spirits

Alsace is renowned for its wines, and the Christmas markets are an excellent place to sample and purchase local varieties. Look for bottles of Riesling, Gewürztraminer, and Crémant d'Alsace. Additionally, you can find locally produced spirits such as schnapps and eaux-de-vie, which make for unique and festive gifts.

 # Christmas Decorations

In addition to ornaments, the markets are filled with a wide range of Christmas decorations. Look for handmade wreaths, nativity scene figurines, and festive table settings. These items can add a touch of Strasbourg's festive spirit to your home.

Artisanal Chocolates

Alsace is known for its high-quality chocolates, and the Christmas markets are a great place to indulge in these sweet treats. Look for artisanal chocolates made by local chocolatiers, often available in beautifully packaged boxes that make perfect gifts.

 ## Scented Candles and Soaps

For a sensory delight, consider purchasing scented candles and soaps. These items are often handmade and come in a variety of festive scents, such as cinnamon, pine, and vanilla. They make lovely gifts or additions to your own home.

 ## Traditional Clothing and Accessories

The markets also offer a selection of traditional Alsatian clothing and accessories. Look for items such as embroidered scarves, woolen hats, and handcrafted jewelry. These pieces are not only stylish but also reflect the rich cultural heritage of the region.

 ## Local Honey and Jams

For a taste of Alsace, consider buying local honey and jams. These products are often made with regional fruits and flowers, resulting in unique and delicious flavors. They make great gifts for food enthusiasts or a sweet treat for yourself.

Tips For Shopping At Strasbourg Christmas Markets

1. BRING CASH: While some vendors may accept credit or debit cards, many prefer cash. It's a good idea to bring enough cash to cover your purchases for the day, as ATMs can be scarce and lines can be long. Having cash on hand ensures you won't miss out on any must-have items.

2. DRESS WARMLY: December in Strasbourg can be quite cold, so dressing in layers is essential. Wear a warm coat, hat, gloves, and scarf to stay comfortable while shopping. Comfortable, waterproof footwear is also a must, as you'll be spending a lot of time walking around.

3. BRING A REUSABLE SHOPPING BAG: Most vendors won't provide bags, or they may only have small ones. Bringing a large, reusable shopping bag will make it easier to carry your purchases and is also an eco-friendly option. Channel your inner Santa and be prepared to lug around your festive finds.

4. DO A LAP BEFORE BUYING:

Before making any purchases, take a walk around the entire market to see what's on offer. This will give you a good idea of the variety of goods available and help you make informed decisions about what to buy. You might find better deals or more unique items by exploring all the stalls first.

5. PLAN YOUR PURCHASES:

Make a list of the items you want to buy and set a budget before you go. This helps you stay on track and avoid buying things on a whim. Having a plan ensures you get everything you need without overspending.

6. ENGAGE WITH THE VENDORS:

Don't hesitate to chat with the vendors. They can provide valuable information about their products and may even offer discounts or special deals. Engaging with the vendors also enhances your shopping experience and gives you a deeper appreciation for the craftsmanship behind the goods.

7. SAMPLE BEFORE YOU BUY:

Many food vendors offer samples of their products. Take advantage of this to try before you buy, ensuring you get the best-tasting treats. This is especially useful for items like cheese, sausages, and sweets.

8. SHOP EARLY OR LATE:

To avoid the busiest times, visit the markets early in the morning or later in the evening. This will give you a more relaxed shopping experience and allow you to browse the stalls without the crowds. Early mornings are also a great time to find freshly made food items.

9. STAY HYDRATED AND TAKE BREAKS:

Shopping at the markets can be tiring, so make sure to stay hydrated and take breaks. Enjoy a warm drink like vin chaud (mulled wine) or hot chocolate to keep your energy up. There are plenty of food stalls where you can sit down and enjoy a snack while taking in the festive atmosphere.

10. KNOW HOW TO SPOT HANDMADE GOODS:

If you want to ensure you're buying authentic, handmade items, look for signs of craftsmanship.

Check for business cards or labels indicating the origin of the product. Be wary of items that seem too cheap, as they may be mass-produced. Authentic handmade goods often come with a higher price tag but are worth the investment for their quality and uniqueness.

11. BE MINDFUL OF YOUR BELONGINGS:

In big crowds, it's crucial to watch your belongings. Use a safe bag or backpack and keep your valuables close to you. Be aware of your surroundings and avoid carrying too much cash or expensive items.

CHAPTER 7

Useful French Phrases For Strasbourg Christmas Markets

Basic Greetings and Politeness

- Bonjour   *Hello / Good morning*

- Bonsoir   *Good evening*

- Merci   *Thank you*

- Merci beaucoup   *Thank you very much*

- S'il vous plaît   *Please*

- Excusez-moi   *Excuse me*

- Désolée   *Sorry*

Shopping And Buying

- Combien ça coûte?   *How much does it cost?*

- Je voudrais acheter...   *I would like to buy...*

- C'est combien?   *How much is it?*

- Pouvez-vous me montrer...? *Can you show me...?*

- Je peux payer par carte? *Can I pay by card?*

- as-tu de la monnaie ?? *Do you have change?*

Food and Drink

- Je voudrais un vin chaud, s'il vous plaît *I would like a mulled wine, please*

- Qu'est-ce que vous recommandez? *What do you recommend?*

- C'est délicieux! *It's delicious!*

- Je suis allergique à... *I am allergic to...*

- Sans gluten *Gluten-free*

- Végétarien *Vegetarian*

- L'addition, s'il vous plaît *The bill, please*

Directions And Assistance

- Où est...? *Where is...?*

- Pouvez-vous m'aider? *Can you help me?*

- À gauche *To the left*

- À droite *To the right*

- Près d'ici   *Near here*

- Tout droit   *Straight ahead*

Compliments

- c'est merveilleux!   *That's wonderful*

- J'adore ce marché   *I love this market*

- Vous avez de beaux produits   *You have beautiful products*

- Joyeux Noël!   *Merry Christmas!*

Emergency

- Appelez une ambulance!   *Call an ambulance!*

- J'ai besoin d'un médecin   *I need a doctor*

- Où est la pharmacie?   *Where is the pharmacy?*

- J'ai perdu mon portefeuille   *I lost my wallet*

CONCLUSION

As we wrap up our festive journey through Strasbourg's Christmas markets, I'd like to extend a heartfelt merci for choosing this guide to accompany you on your adventure. From the twinkling lights of Place Broglie to the aromatic allure of vin chaud at Place Kléber, we've explored the magical stalls and hidden corners that make these markets a winter wonderland.

I hope this book has not only served as your guide but also as a warm, festive sweater, enveloping you with joy and the sweet scent of gingerbread. Whether you ventured through the pages from the comfort of your home or navigated the cobbled streets of Strasbourg in person, thank you for letting me be a part of your holiday season.

As you close this book, may your spirits be as light as a snowflake and your heart as full as a Christmas stocking. And remember, no matter how many cookies you've indulged in at the markets, dancing around the Christmas tree is an excellent workout.

Wishing you a season filled with peace, joy, and perhaps a touch of Alsatian magic. Until next time, keep your mittens ready and your spirits bright!

Happy Holidays!!! 🎄 ✨

BONUS SECTION:

Christmas Shopping Planner

THIS CHRISTMAS
SHOPPING PLANNER

Belongs to:

....

....

My Christmas
SHOPPING PLANNER

DATE: _____

THINGS TO BUY	BUDGET	ACTUAL PRICE

My Christmas
SHOPPING PLANNER

DATE: _____

THINGS TO BUY	BUDGET	ACTUAL PRICE

My Christmas
SHOPPING PLANNER

DATE: —————————

THINGS TO BUY	BUDGET	ACTUAL PRICE

My Christmas
SHOPPING PLANNER

DATE: —————————

THINGS TO BUY	BUDGET	ACTUAL PRICE

My Christmas
SHOPPING PLANNER

THINGS TO BUY	BUDGET	ACTUAL PRICE

My Christmas
SHOPPING PLANNER

DATE: _____

THINGS TO BUY	BUDGET	ACTUAL PRICE

My Christmas
SHOPPING PLANNER

DATE: _____

THINGS TO BUY	BUDGET	ACTUAL PRICE

My Christmas
SHOPPING PLANNER

DATE: _____

THINGS TO BUY	BUDGET	ACTUAL PRICE

My Christmas
SHOPPING PLANNER

DATE: _____

THINGS TO BUY	BUDGET	ACTUAL PRICE

My Christmas
SHOPPING PLANNER

DATE: _____

THINGS TO BUY	BUDGET	ACTUAL PRICE

NOTE:

NOTE:

NOTE:

Made in United States
Orlando, FL
07 November 2024

53563616R00046